With compliments from Congressman Darrell Issa and the Library of Congress

Pazienza Pizza

Gabrielle Mercedes Cinelli

PAZIENZA PIZZA

Copyright © 2020 Gabrielle Mercedes Cinelli

1405 SW 6th Avenue • Ocala, Florida 34471 • Phone 352-622-1825 • Fax 352-622-1875
Website: www.atlantic-pub.com • Email: sales@atlantic-pub.com
SAN Number: 268-1250

No part of this publication may be reproduced, stored in a retrieval system, or transmitted in any form or by any means, electronic, mechanical, photocopying, recording, scanning, or otherwise, except as permitted under Section 107 or 108 of the 1976 United States Copyright Act, without the prior written permission of the Publisher. Requests to the Publisher for permission should be sent to Atlantic Publishing Group, Inc., 1405 SW 6th Avenue, Ocala, Florida 34471.

Library of Congress Control Number: 2020914896

LIMIT OF LIABILITY/DISCLAIMER OF WARRANTY: The publisher and the author make no representations or warranties with respect to the accuracy or completeness of the contents of this work and specifically disclaim all warranties, including without limitation warranties of fitness for a particular purpose. No warranty may be created or extended by sales or promotional materials. The advice and strategies contained herein may not be suitable for every situation. This work is sold with the understanding that the publisher is not engaged in rendering legal, accounting, or other professional services. If professional assistance is required, the services of a competent professional should be sought. Neither the publisher nor the author shall be liable for damages arising herefrom. The fact that an organization or Web site is referred to in this work as a citation and/or a potential source of further information does not mean that the author or the publisher endorses the information the organization or Web site may provide or recommendations it may make. Further, readers should be aware that Internet Web sites listed in this work may have changed or disappeared between when this work was written and when it is read.

TRADEMARK DISCLAIMER: All trademarks, trade names, or logos mentioned or used are the property of their respective owners and are used only to directly describe the products being provided. Every effort has been made to properly capitalize, punctuate, identify, and attribute trademarks and trade names to their respective owners, including the use of ® and ™ wherever possible and practical. Atlantic Publishing Group, Inc. is not a partner, affiliate, or licensee with the holders of said trademarks.

This is a work of fiction. Names, characters, businesses, places, events, locales, and incidents are either the products of the author's imagination or used in a fictitious manner. Any resemblance to actual persons, living or dead, or actual events is purely coincidental.

Printed in the United States

PROJECT MANAGER: Katie Cline
INTERIOR LAYOUT AND JACKET DESIGN: Nicole Sturk

Dedicated to Nini.

Writing this made me feel as though I was picking green beans with you again.

At school on Friday, I was counting the seconds until the dismissal bell rang. I love school, but I couldn't wait to start my special weekend. When I glanced out the window, I saw Nonna walking down the street.

BRRRINNNGGG! Finally, the day was over! I rushed out with the rest of the class, dashed across the lawn, and threw my arms around Nonna. She scooped me up into a tight hug. Nonna always gave the very best hugs.

"**Ciao**, Anna," she chuckled.

"**Ciao**, Nonna!" I exclaimed with my face smooshed right up against hers. We turned to start our walk to her house. *The second we walked through the door,* I thought, *I am racing to the kitchen and starting to make that pizza!*

When we got to the house, I rushed over to the counter and began pulling out measuring spoons and bowls, but Nonna stopped me and beckoned me to the table. She pulled out a piece of paper and a pencil.

"First, we need to make a list, so we can pick up all of our ingredients tomorrow," Nonna explained.

Tomorrow? I thought, deflating.

Together, we wrote down all of the ingredients we'd need for the pizza. Since it was my favorite food, I knew everything we had to get. My pencil flew across the page as if writing quickly would make tomorrow arrive sooner.

When I announced that I was done, Nonna picked up the pencil and crossed out "basil" and "tomatoes." A huge smile spread across my face, and I raced to change into my gardening clothes before rushing out to the backyard.

Nonna was waiting for me, wearing her gardening gloves, just like she had when she worked on her farm in Italy. She held up a pair for me, and I squealed in excitement.

As I pulled on my gloves, I heard Nini from behind the tomato plants say, "We only have a few more hours before the sun goes down and a lot of tomatoes to pick!"

I giggled and hurried over to give him a hug before the three of us got to work. Once we'd picked enough of the reddest, plumpest, juiciest tomatoes for our sauce, we moved over to the basil plants.

SNIFF, SNAP! SNIFF, SNIP! SNIFF, SNAP! The snipping of fresh basil always brought a smile to my face.

"Let's get cooking!" I exclaimed with a basketful of basil.

"Not so fast, Anna. We will start cooking tomorrow," Nonna reminded me. I'd hoped she'd forgotten.

In the morning I awoke to a mouthwatering aroma of tomatoes, basil, garlic, and Italian herbs simmering. Nonna's sauce was cooking. I sprang up, brushed my teeth, threw on some clothes, and flew downstairs to start the day.

We went to the Italian market in town and picked up the ingredients we needed. Then we spent the rest of the day finishing and jarring Nonna's sauce. As we finished up, I glanced at the clock to see that it was already 3:18!

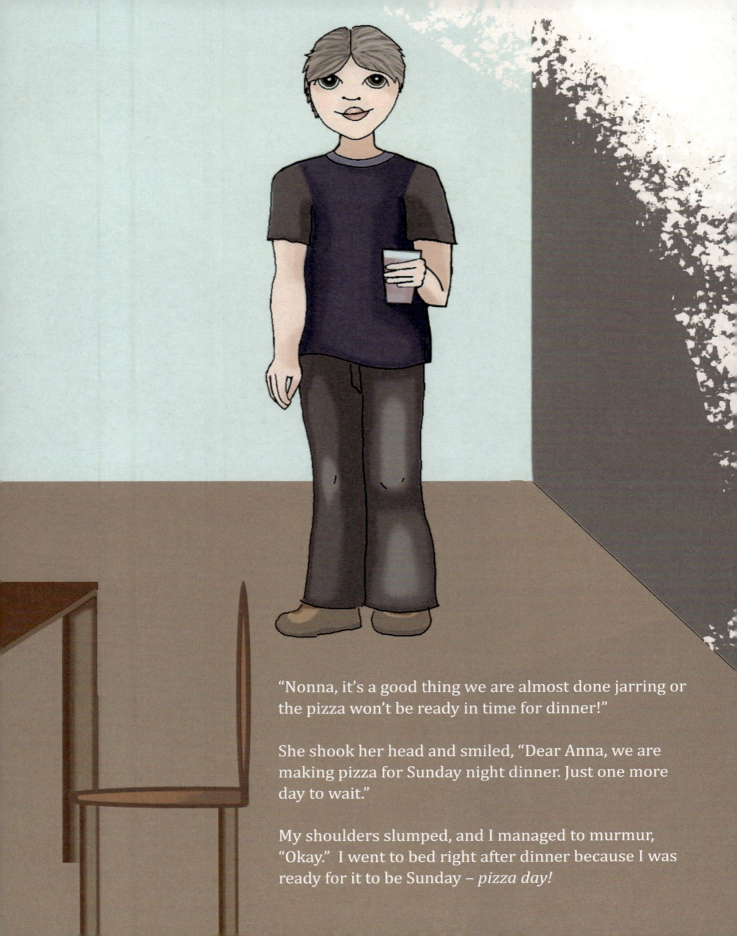

"Nonna, it's a good thing we are almost done jarring or the pizza won't be ready in time for dinner!"

She shook her head and smiled, "Dear Anna, we are making pizza for Sunday night dinner. Just one more day to wait."

My shoulders slumped, and I managed to murmur, "Okay." I went to bed right after dinner because I was ready for it to be Sunday – *pizza day!*

The next morning, I threw on my cooking apron and bandana and hurried down the stairs and greeted Nonna and Nini with a smile. "I'm ready to get started!"

Nonna chuckled, "I know you're excited, dear, but it only takes an hour and a half to make pizza, and dinner isn't until five. We won't be starting for a while!"

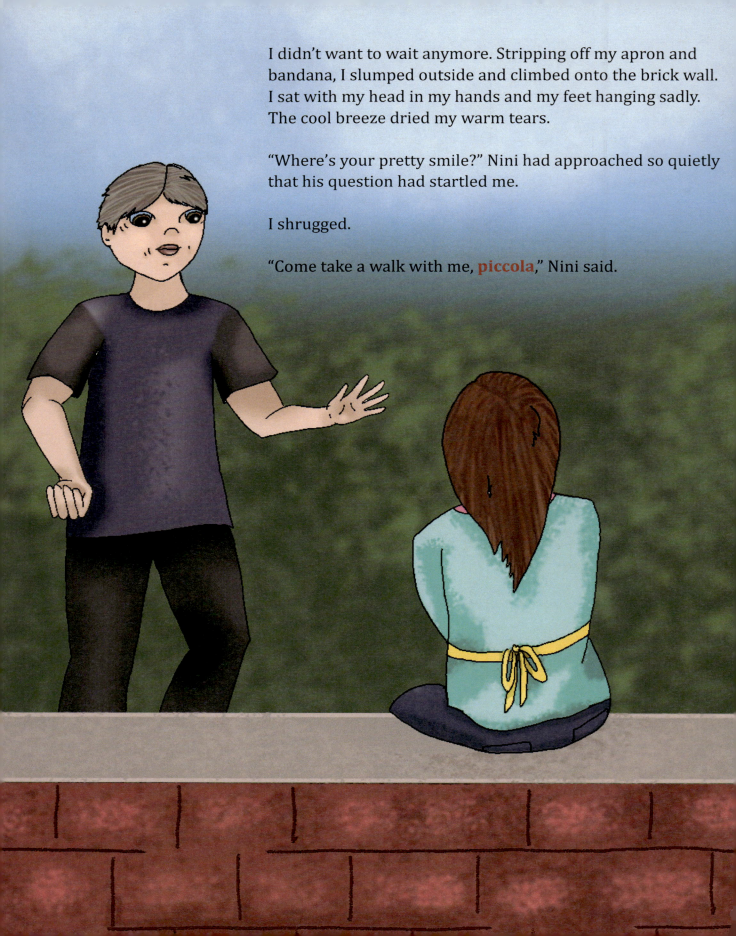

I didn't want to wait anymore. Stripping off my apron and bandana, I slumped outside and climbed onto the brick wall. I sat with my head in my hands and my feet hanging sadly. The cool breeze dried my warm tears.

"Where's your pretty smile?" Nini had approached so quietly that his question had startled me.

I shrugged.

"Come take a walk with me, **piccola**," Nini said.

We ended up by the wooden trellises where Nini's green beans grow. "Do you know why green beans are my favorite vegetable, Anna?" he started.

"No, but they're my favorite too," I said.

"They're my favorite because green beans taste the best when they are picked at just the right time. It can take fourteen weeks! Then you have to check them every day to see if they've reached perfection. But in the end, the wait is always worth it."

He put his arm around my shoulder, and we continued down the row of vines that would eventually yield the perfect beans. When we got to the end of the row, I hugged him and smiled. "I love you, Nini. Let's go inside and see what Nonna is up to."

"Good idea, **piccola**!"

All of the ingredients were set up on the counter when we came back inside. Nonna was washing the pizza stones. I went over and picked up a rag to help her dry them. She looked down at me and smiled.

"I'm sorry for getting upset, Nonna," I said.

"That's okay, **bella**, I know you're just excited. Patience is very important while cooking. The best meals take time."

"I know, Nonna. That's why I'm the amateur, and you're the expert!" I joked.

We both laughed and sat down to snack on some **espresso** and **biscotti**.

As we ate, Nonna told me that she went ahead and made the dough while I was in the garden with Nini, so we wouldn't fall behind schedule.

"You will have to teach me how to make the dough another time, Nonna," I said.

"Of course!" she agreed. "All right, my dear, are you ready to learn the recipe?"

"Of course I'm ready!"

I grabbed the blank recipe card and came back to sit at the table. At the top of the card, in my neatest handwriting, I wrote: Nonna's Pizza. Suddenly, I didn't mind going slowly. Nonna, in her big, beautiful accent, dictated the steps to making the pizza while I wrote them down on the card beneath the ingredients.

Once the recipe was written on the card, we were ready to cook! But before we got started, we both washed our hands thoroughly.

After our hands were clean and dry, we spread the dough on our round pizza stones.

Next, we poured some olive oil on the dough and used a spoon to spread it around. "The olive oil helps to make the dough nice and crispy," Nonna explained as she preheated the oven to 450 degrees. Next, we used a ladle to spread some of the sauce we'd made yesterday onto the dough. Once we finished spreading the sauce, it was time to add the mozzarella cheese. We sprinkled it on each of our pies, using plenty!

BEEP. BEEP. BEEP. The oven was ready. We added a final touch: a fresh basil leaf in the center. I watched as Nonna placed our pizzas in the oven. She carefully placed my pizza on the top rack and hers on the bottom rack. "Now we wait," Nonna said.

"Now we wait," I repeated with a smile, nodding.

DING, DONG! The doorbell announced that our whole family had arrived for Sunday dinner. As my mom, dad, aunt, and cousins walked in, they remarked about how good it smelled. I was beaming from ear to ear.

Everyone gathered around the table. When the timer buzzed, Nonna pulled the pizzas out to cool. My mouth was watering as I stared wide-eyed at my pizza.

After cutting the pizzas into slices, Nonna proclaimed, "**Mangiare**!" welcoming us to dig in. But instead of rushing to eat, I watched everyone else take their first bite.

"You made this, Anna?" my mom asked after wiping my pizza's sauce from her mouth. "It's just as good as your Nonna's!"

I felt so proud of making my very own pizza. Nini and Nonna smiled at me. My teeth finally sunk into the gooey cheese and the sweet crust. After swallowing, I announced, "This pizza was definitely worth the wait!"

Nonna, Nini, and I laughed as everyone continued to enjoy the delicious pizza. We gobbled up every last slice!

After dinner, it was time to go home with Mom and Dad. Even though waiting for the pizza seemed to take forever, I realized that the weekend had flown by. It felt like it was too soon to leave. I wrapped my arms around Nonna and Nini, squeezing them tight.

"This was the best weekend ever!" I said.

"How about we make **zeppole** next time, bella?" Nonna suggested.

"Great idea, Nonna!" I agreed. "I'll have to be patient waiting for next time because a good cook is always patient, and good things are worth the wait."

We shared one last hug, and I left with a smile, a full belly, and a happy heart thinking about my next visit with Nonna and Nini.

Nonna's Pizza

Ingredients:

Dough
1 cup mozzarella cheese
½ cup tomato sauce (homemade preferably)
1 tbs. Italian seasoning
1 tbs. garlic powder
½ tbs. salt
2 tbs. olive oil
1 or 2 Basil leaves

Directions:

1. Preheat oven to 450 degrees Fahrenheit.
2. Smooth the dough into a circle on a pan or pizza stone.
3. Evenly spread the olive oil over the dough using a spoon.
4. Evenly spread the tomato sauce over the oiled dough using a spoon. Leave ½ an inch to an inch of space at the edge of the crust.
5. Sprinkle the garlic powder, salt, and Italian seasoning over the sauce.
6. Sprinkle the mozzarella cheese evenly across the pizza leaving ½ an inch to an inch of space at the edge of the crust.
7. Place a basil leaf in the middle of the pizza.
8. Carefully place the pizza in the middle rack of your oven.
9. Bake for 25 minutes or until the crust is a light golden-brown.
10. Remove, cool, and carefully cut.
11. Enjoy!